A BRIEF HISTORY OF JERSEY

by
Peter Hunt

SOCIÉTÉ JERSIAISE

1998

i

By the same author:
A Guide to the Dolmens of Jersey

The author would like to thank and acknowledge the contributions made by the following. **Text editing:** A. Podger, Mrs P. Taylor, C. N. Aubin, R. Nichols, Mrs M. Backhurst, Miss L. Holt, Dr J. Renouf, R. Long, Mrs M. Long. **For photographic research:** D. Umney, Miss M. Billot and Miss S. Knight. With thanks, for her unflagging support, Mrs Jenny Hunt.

Front and back cover photograph of St Ouen's Manor by Gareth Syvret.

Photographic acknowledgement and permission: Dr J. Renouf (Rybot's map of Jersey); Jersey Tourism (States building, Lieutenant-Governor, Grosnez Castle, Jersey cow, La Corbière lighthouse, States at Gorey); Société Jersiaise archives (Royal Court, Sir George Carteret, the trench plough, General Don, Victoria College, Queen's visit 1989, air terminal, wartime queues, Jersey railway, S.S. *Vega*). Jersey Evening Post (Queen's visit 1989); John Jean (steam packet, Jersey potatoes, oyster boats). Gareth Syvret (La Cotte, Le Pinacle, Hermitage Rock). Jersey Museums Service (La Hougue Bie, gold torque, Mont Orgueil, cider press, Elizabeth Castle). Jersey Archive Service (Charter of 1341, D/AP/B/2; By courtesy of the National Portrait Gallery (Sir Walter Raleigh, John Wesley); Bundesarchiv (German fortifications); Tate Gallery (Death of Major Peirson, Battle of Jersey, by J. S. Copley); National Arts Museum of Sweden (M. Luther by Lucas Cranach).

ISBN 0 901897 22 1

Contents

SOCIÉTÉ JERSIAISE

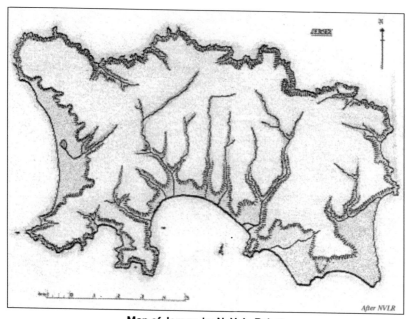

Map of Jersey, by N. V. L. Rybot

After NVLR

Introduction

THE Channel Islands are termed a 'Peculiar of the Crown'. They owe their allegiance directly to the English Crown, not to the Parliament of the United Kingdom. This is because they are the last remaining territories of the Dukes of Normandy of whom William of Normandy conquered England in 1066, thereby becoming King William I of England. The Islands' loyalty, therefore, is to their first Liege Lords, the Dukes of Normandy and, through them, directly to the English Crown.

The Channel Islands consists of two Bailiwicks, or areas under the guidance of a Bailiff — the chief civil official. One Bailiwick comprises Guernsey, Alderney, Sark and the smaller islands, the other is Jersey with its off-shore reefs Les Minquiers and Les Écréhous.

Jersey is the largest of the Channel Islands and the most southerly.

It is irregular in shape being about 9 miles by 5 miles or 45 square miles in area. It is formed primarily from granite giving it an imposing and rocky coastline.

Through its position in the gulf of St Malo, it is also subject to dramatic tidal ranges. For these natural reasons it has been a difficult island to conquer.

Historically, its geographical position made it an important outpost for England. In the Medieval period it lay on the route of the important wine and salt trades which ran from Gascony in the south-west of France to England in the north. Later, it was to be of strategic importance. Being only 12 miles from the shores of France, it became a base for smugglers and privateers during the many wars against the French.

It has suffered from invasions by Bretons, Saxons, Gauls, Vikings, Romans, French, Germans and, during the English Civil War of the 17th century, from the English Parliamentarians as well.

It has seen internecine strife, violent political feuds and serious economic problems. It has felt the impact of Catholicism, Calvinism, Methodism and Anglicanism as well as surviving radical changes to its social structure.

Its languages have included Latin, Breton, Norman French, Jersey Norman French, French and English. Well into the 1900s, many inhabitants would be tri-lingual though the rural communities were more likely to speak Jèrriais (Jersey French) or French — for this reason the Book of Common Prayer had to be translated into French for the majority of the population.

Despite this, or maybe because of it, the Island has developed its own character — neither English nor French — and encapsulated in this 45 square miles is a vibrant history as one of the 'Peculiars of the English Crown'.

The façade of the States building

The Governance of Jersey

THE Island of Jersey is divided into 12 parishes, each parish being a civic and ecclesiastical centre for its inhabitants.

Each parish is run by an elected Constable who is the 'Father' of the parish. He or she with the Parish Assembly sets the parish rates, initially raised to support the poor of the parish, runs the parish budget, heads the Honorary Police Force with its age-old officers of Centenier and Vingtenier, settles local disputes and, formerly, had the power to enlist men into the Militia.

The Constable takes a seat in the Jersey States or Parliament. Each parish, depending on its population, elects one or more Deputies to the States as its local States members.

Though nowadays the professional police are responsible for policing the Island, the honorary police still play a role in policing their own parishes and are required by the legal system to present all cases in the central Police Court.

The third parish figure of importance, though his powers are less in modern times, is the Rector of the Anglican Church. As well as parochial duties, the Rector undertakes civic duties. He presides over the Parish Ecclesiastical Assembly which elects church officials, maintains the Parish Church, Rectory and Cemetery as well as sitting on committees that deal with community matters. However, half the parishes no longer have a Rector but a Priest-in-Charge and more changes are imminent.

The insular Parliament, the States, evolved from the Royal Court, in early times the only legislative assembly. It began by being a consultative body to the Royal Court but developed into being the legislative body whereas the Royal Court remained the judicial body. The States earliest surviving Acte dates from 1524.

The Bailiff sits in the Royal Court as Chief Judge of Law assisted by 12 Jurats or Judges of Fact chosen by an electoral college. They are now supported and assisted by the Deputy Bailiff, the Attorney-General, the Solicitor-General, (both Crown appointments), the Judicial

The Royal Court

Greffier (the Clerk of the Court) and the Vicomte (the executive officer). Though its origins can be traced back to the 13th century, the Royal Court has undergone several changes during the last 100 years.

The composition of the States, on the other hand, has changed considerably from its early days. Probably based on the model of the French Trois États, it represented the three estates of Nobility, Church and Bourgeoisie. These estates were represented by the 12 Jurats, the 12 Rectors and the 12 Constables. Nowadays the Jurats and the Rectors no longer sit in the States — the assembly being formed by the Constables, the Deputies and 12 Senators — all elected by popular franchise.

The Bailiff presides over both the Royal Court and the States. The States may not sit without the permission of the Lieutenant-Governor, although this is now largely a formality. He and the Dean of Jersey both have a voice in the States but have no vote. The work of the States is managed by the office of the Greffier or Clerk of the States supported by the Island's civil service.

The Crown, through its Privy Council, is ultimately responsible for

General Sir Michael Wilkes, Lieutenant-Governor, at Mont Orgueil in 1996

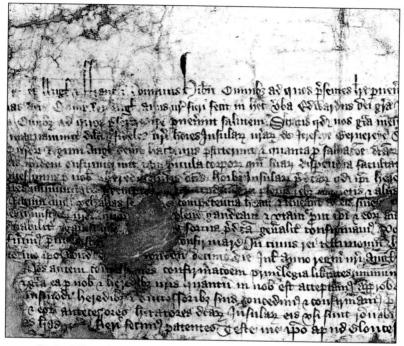

Part of the original charter of 1341 (Jersey Archives Service)

the safety of its Jersey subjects but Jersey can legislate for all its internal affairs subject to permanent laws being approved by the Crown-in-Council. The Island's point of contact in the British Parliament is the Home Secretary, a Privy Councillor, who replies on behalf of the Crown to questions in Parliament that relate to Island affairs.

The Crown is represented in the Island by a Lieutenant-Governor. His role is now mainly ceremonial, although he has certain responsibilities relating to immigration and he may attend States meetings, but has no vote. The development of the power of the States and the judiciary have replaced the authority held at certain times by the Governor and earlier by the Wardens and Lords of the Isles.

The Channel Islands have been governed by the laws of Normandy and their own local customs and, more recently, by Statute Law. Following the loss of Normandy by King John in 1204, he may have modified the Island's laws by the 'Constitutions of King John', but no text survives. During the 13th and early 14th centuries disputes arose as to the governance of the Island, but in 1341 Edward III confirmed by charter the Island's privileges, liberties and customs in general terms.

These privileges were successfully confirmed by each monarch until the end of the 17th century; the last charter being that of James II in 1687. Since then, the rights of the Islanders have been acknowledged by other means.

Jersey has taken full advantage of its tariff-free status and its geographical position throughout its history.

The Prehistoric Age in Jersey

IN the Old Stone Age (Palaeolithic) people occupied cave dwellings in Jersey, the most famous being La Cotte de Saint Brelade where the first known occupation is over 200,000 years old.

Changes of sea-level, due to the melting of Arctic ice, caused the cave and probably the Island to be abandoned for a long period before being reoccupied some 100,000 years ago.

This was the era of the Neanderthal people and 13 human teeth have been excavated from this period which are now in the Jersey Museum.

The entrance to the cave at La Cotte, St Brelade

The entrance to the tomb at La Hougue Bie, Grouville

The New Stone Age (Neolithic) people came to Jersey around 4000 BC and among finds of this period are querns for grinding corn, pottery, axes and flint fragments — enough evidence to suggest permanent occupation. A feature of this period was the construction of stone monuments, known locally as dolmens and menhirs, some of which have miraculously survived to this day.

There are ten excellent examples on the Island, the most outstanding being La Hougue Bie in the parish of Grouville. It is in excellent condition, covered by an impressive mound and surmounted by two chapels, one from the 12th century and one probably from the late 15th century.

Remains have also been found from the succeeding Bronze and Iron Ages, the most spectacular discovery being a gold torque, a long ornament of twisted gold, which is exhibited in the Jersey Museum.

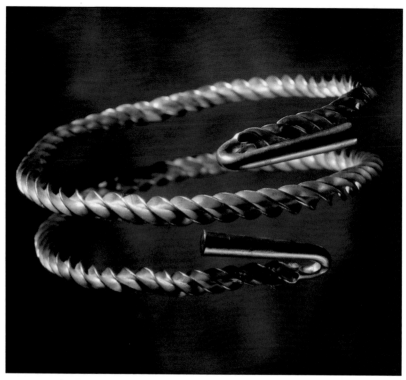

The gold torque, on view in the Jersey Museum

In the first century BC, towards the close of the Iron Age, the areas adjacent to the Channel Islands in France were settled by the Gaulish tribes. As the might of Rome advanced north, groups of these Gauls fled to the Channel Islands in the hope of establishing their homes away from the influence of Rome. Many coins have been discovered from their time of settlement.

Of the Roman period there is surprisingly little evidence. Remains of a Gallo-Roman shrine exist at the Pinnacle site on the north-western cliffs and a broken pillar, twice re-used in later times, was found under the floor of St Lawrence's Church. However, as it is not made of local granite, no one can say how or when it came to Jersey. Roman coins have been found in fair numbers but as they were universal throughout Western Europe this is not surprising.

The Pinnacle Rock, St Ouen

Christianity came to Jersey from the north-west, brought by Britons escaping from the Anglo-Saxon encroachment through the south and west of England. These Britons established themselves in Armorica, now known as Brittany.

It is believed that St Marcouf was the first missionary to teach Christianity in Jersey in about AD 540, although St Sampson preached in Guernsey and is known to have visited Jersey on his way to Dol in Brittany whose Bishop he became.

The most revered of the early Christians is an anchorite called Helibert who established himself in a cave on what is now called the Hermitage Rock. Tradition has it that he was murdered by pirates in AD 555. He is now known as St Helier and has given his name to Jersey's capital town.

The Hermitage rock, home of St Helier

Contrary to popular belief it is unlikely that Caesarea was the early name for Jersey. About AD 285 the Antonine Itinerary listed 15 islands and it is believed that Jersey was then called Andium. With the Breton influence, it is probable that it was renamed Angia, a Breton name denoting a large island. The most likely development of the name Jersey is from the Norse. In Norse the suffix '-ey' means island and it is thought that 'Geirr' as it was written was the name of a Norse pirate chieftain who conquered the Island from the Bretons around AD 800.

Whatever its maverick beginnings, it has been known from Norman times as Jersey, despite various spellings, as indeed has its sister island been known as Guernsey.

Feudalism and the Middle Ages

DURING the ninth century AD a major influence was the migration of the Vikings or Norsemen south. Though warlike and militarily well organised, they began to develop settlements first along the coast and then extending inland. In 911, Charles the Simple of France legitimised the inevitable by ceding to Rollo the province now known as Normandy, the main area in which the Norsemen had settled.

Rollo's son, William Longsword, annexed the Cotentin peninsula and the Channel Islands into the Duchy of Normandy. The Normans soon lost their Scandinavian customs, adopting the French language and Christianity, as well as developing their own laws, known later as the Grand Coutumier.

Feudalism and the seigneurial system flourished in Jersey from this time. All land was claimed by the Duke which he granted to his favourites in return for service and rentes, a form of mortgage. They became the seigneurs, owing allegiance to the Duke and, in turn, demanding allegiance from their tenants. Land was also granted to religious houses in return for the offices required for the good of the Duke's soul and for the souls of the donors and their families.

Tenants paid rent, gave a tenth of their crop (a tithe) to the church and worked for an agreed number of days on their seigneur's land. The seigneurs were responsible for the mills and a proportion of their tenants' crops would be their due. Wheat was the main crop and products made from flour, with the addition of locally caught fish, were the staple diet. In fact, wheat or its value continued to be the basis of currency and valuation of worth up to the present century. In return, the seigneur held a court to settle local disputes and it was his duty to raise arms to protect his lands.

There remains to this day, still occasionally used, a cry for help to the Grand Seigneur. It is called the clameur de Haro — an appeal to one's supreme lord for redress.

GUILLAUME

LE CONQUÉRANT.

William the Conqueror

Mont Orgueil and Gorey harbour

On being wronged, the injured party calls out 'Haro, Haro, Haro, A l'aide mon Prince. On me fait tort' ('Help me, my Prince, I am being wronged'). The aggressor must desist his action until the matter is resolved in Court.

It is thought that the 'Haro' could mean a direct appeal to Rollo, the first Duke of Normandy, 'Hail, Rollo' but the cry may just be an old call for help.

The seigneurs have played a vital role in the history of Jersey. Some were highly influential in keeping the Island loyal to the English monarchs during the wars with France and, later, through the de Carteret family in particular, ensured that the Island stayed Royalist during the English civil war even though the sympathies of the majority of the population were with the Parliamentarians.

In Jersey, there were over 100 fiefs, each with its own seigneur. Most seigneurial rights were not abolished until as late as 1966 and, even now, fiefs and some limited seigneurial rights remain..

It is unlikely that the conquest of England by William, Duke of Normandy, in 1066 involved the Channel Islanders. Certainly Wace, the Jersey-born Norman poet, does not mention any Jerseymen being involved.

Island life was in farming the land, mainly by small-holdings and in fishing. Up to the Reformation, when Catholic days of fasting were many, Jersey benefited from waters full of conger eel, fish and shellfish.

However, in 1204, the status of the Island was to change for ever. King John lost Normandy to the French King and, suddenly, the coast of France, just 12 miles away, became enemy territory.

The landowners had to decide whether to give up their estates in Normandy and keep their estates in Jersey, or vice versa. Those who left lost their land to the Crown who often granted it to new owners. The decision to go or stay would in all likelihood have been made on the basis of understandable self-interest.

A strange anomaly occurred in that Jersey, which fell under the Catholic diocese of Coutances in Normandy, remained part of this diocese until 1569, well into the reign of Elizabeth I and the establishment of the Church of England, despite formal Papal Bulls of 1496 and 1499. It then became a part of the diocese of Winchester and remains in that diocese to this day.

It is from the 13th century that Mont Orgueil castle dates and it has proved most useful. Major attacks on Jersey by the French came in 1214, 1294, 1338, 1373 (led by Bertrand du Guescelin, Marshal of France, the foremost soldier of his time), 1380, 1403 and 1406. These attacks were unsuccessful but, in 1461, Jersey was attacked by the Count de Maulevrier who took Mont Orgueil and held the Island for the French for seven years until it was relieved by the English under Sir Richard Harliston.

It was during this period that the Island government institutions were confirmed and the embryonic structure of the States, of Bailiff, Jurats, Constables and Rectors was further developed.

The remains of Grosnez Castle, St Ouen

It was also during this period that Grosnez Castle in the north-west was built as a temporary shelter against these frequent attacks. It remained in use from the late 13th century until the 15th century.

Life for the Islanders could be appalling. In 1339 the Island was effectively razed to the ground, three times in all, by the invading French. Conditions became so bad that, at the request of Edward IV in 1481, the Pope issued a Papal Bull of Neutrality. This placed the Channel Islands under the protection of the Church, hostilities being prohibited so long as the islands remained in sight.

This was welcomed in particular by the ecclesiastical authorities as they maintained property and influence in the islands. It also benefited the Islanders in that they could now trade with both sides during outbreaks of hostilities in the Hundred Years War.

This privilege of neutrality lasted for 200 years until 1689 when William III in his bitter fight with Louis XIV would not countenance any trade with the enemy.

However, there was an even worse disaster about to descend on Europe in the 1340s — the Black Death. Though no accurate figure of how many died is known, modern historians accept Froissart's estimate that a third of the world's population perished. The Channel Islands suffered the same fate as their contemporaries and there is a distinct possibility that the plague was carried from France to England by the Channel Island traders.

The twin activities of farming and sea trading, developed from the 11th to the 15th century, were to stand the Island in good stead on the discovery of the New World at the end of the 15th century; and, at home, a cottage industry of knitting was about to become a source of considerable wealth to the Island's small-holding community.

The Tudors

IN 1485 Henry Tudor defeated Richard III at the Battle of Bosworth and became King Henry VII. It is generally accepted that Henry's reign saw the end of the Middle Ages and the start of modern history. It was an extraordinary age.

The Renaissance emerged in Italy in the 15th century. With the development of the printing press by Gutenberg, learning and education were no longer the prerogative of the Church and the few.

In 1492 Columbus set sail westward, hoping to reach India. Soon afterwards Magellan circumnavigated the globe. In 1497 Cabot reached Newfoundland. These pioneers were followed by men such as Cortes, Pisarro, Drake, Raleigh, Hawkins and Hudson going west. Following in the footsteps of Marco Polo, although by the longer sea route around Africa, Diaz and Vasco da Gama sailed east.

In the 16th century, nationalism became an ideal under Henry VII of England, Francis of France and Ferdinand of Spain. Sea power and sea trading, particularly with the Orient and later with the New World, created the new wealth of the merchant classes.

The feudal structure of society was in the process of breaking down. Jersey developed to meet these changing times although the seigneurial system remained the basis of the Island's social structure. The small-holding farmer, enclosing his land, continued to eke out an existence for himself and his immediate family, paying his feudal dues.

The major influence at this time on Jersey's traditional life was the upheaval caused by Martin Luther when, in 1517, by questioning the authority of the Catholic Church to sell indulgences, he sparked off the Reformation and the birth of Protestantism.

The growth of Protestantism slowly encroached on one of Jersey's traditional industries, that of fishing. Catholic tradition held fasting as a necessity for the good of the soul. Fish, rather than meat, had to be eaten. The Reformation eventually swept away this tradition.

Fortunately, however, at about this time, a new source of income

Sir Walter Raleigh

from fishing had been discovered in the great cod banks off Newfoundland.

In the mid 1500s an annual pattern developed for the sailors of western Europe which later included Jerseymen. In the spring they would set sail for the fishing grounds off Newfoundland, catch and salt the dry fish and sail south to Spain or Portugal to sell their catch, returning in time for the autumn ploughing.

Southampton became the central port for the merchant sailors of the South of England. For the Jersey fleets, their own harbours being non-existent at this time although the maritime centre in Jersey was St Aubin, wintered in the safe haven of St Malo in France.

In 1549, in England, the Act of Uniformity banned all Latin services. The Book of Common Prayer became the basis of the Church of

St Aubin's Fort

26

Martin Luther, by Lucas Cranach

England's service. In Jersey, this was of little use in the rural communities as they spoke no English. Moreover, Protestantism appealed to the independent nature of the islanders and they adopted wholeheartedly the teachings of Calvin, particularly as his 'Prières Ecclésiastique' was published in French.

In 1553 the Book of Common Prayer was translated into French and came into use in the Island's Anglican churches.

It is during this period that Jersey created an industry which was to last until the early 19th century — that of knitting. Though nowadays the Island is famous for its knitted jersey, the industry created the major part of its income from the production of stockings.

Virtually everyone on the Island was involved in this industry. So much so that, from time to time, the Royal Court issued laws banning knitting at the time of harvesting and when vraic or seaweed (a major source of fuel and fertiliser) was being collected.

The Reformation was to have a further influence on Island life. In 1572 the French Catholics went on the rampage in Paris against the French Calvinists or Huguenots, which began with the Massacre of St Bartholomew's Day. Many Huguenots fled to Jersey bringing their skills with them. A second influx of Huguenots came in 1685 when a further purge was made against them after the Revocation of the Edict of Nantes.

The reign of Elizabeth I (1558-1603) saw Spain, rather than France, as the enemy. Defence of the islands again became imperative and, in 1542, the construction began of St Aubin's fort to be followed in 1590 by Elizabeth Castle, the two to defend the great sweep of St Aubin's Bay — the centre of Jersey's maritime life.

Sir Walter Raleigh held the Governorship of the Islands from 1600 to 1604 and it is possible, although unlikely, that he introduced tobacco to the Island as well as encouraging fishing in Newfoundland. Tobacco flourished so much that a decree was issued in 1628 ordering the tobacco crop to be rooted out.

In 1602, the land registry recording all transactions relating to real property was created. It is in use to this day.

The Stuarts and the English Civil War

DURING the reign of the Stuarts the population of Jersey is estimated to have been between 15,000 and 20,000. The exact number of houses in 1685 is known. It was 3,069.

The basis of society was still seigneurial in that the wealth and the power were in the hands of the leading families.

These families continued to farms their lands but were well educated — usually at Oxford — using English as their main language. They were well versed in the ways of the English Court, in particular with the Privy Council responsible for the affairs of Jersey. From this class came many of the Jurats, the Bailiffs, the officers in the Militia and the merchant adventurers.

However, the smaller farmers, a feature of their fields being their enclosure by high earthen banks topped with hawthorn hedges, were also influential in the political and legal affairs of the Island. They controlled local parish affairs through the Honorary Police system and also had the opportunity to be elected as Jurats and Constables.

The problem for many of the smaller farmers was two-fold. Because of the Norman laws of inheritance and the smallness of their farms, few could support more than the eldest son and his family. Younger sons must take to the sea.

By the time of the Stuarts, the major agricultural crop was apples, grown for production into cider — the drink of both rich and poor — as well as wheat and root crops such as turnips and potatoes. Meat came from their sheep, cattle, pigs and poultry. Their sheep were also a source of wool for the knitting industry, but such was the demand for wool that a majority of the raw material had to be imported from England.

To the local society of the farming and business community and the artisans and labourers must be added the military garrisons, all on temporary assignment and mainly from England or Ireland, stationed at Mont Orgueil or Elizabeth Castle. However, all Jerseymen

The cider press at Hamptonne, Jersey's country life museum

had to do their military service, unpaid, and by 1620 there were three regiments of all-Island militia.

The final group were the poor. Contemporary historians comment on the number of poor in Jersey for the lot of a man without land or position in those times throughout Europe was indeed hard and, in Jersey, where the control of land was through inheritance, there was little opportunity to acquire it unless with wealth created from sources other than the land. Those who were so affected were positively encouraged to emigrate to the new colonies of North America.

This was an era in which the people of Jersey began to take greater control of their own affairs, particularly in the establishment of the authority of the Bailiff over that of the Governor, a feud that lasted

Elizabeth Castle guardien, David Lewis, in ceremonial uniform

Islanders at the harbour waiting to greet Queen Victoria on her arrival in 1846.

This was the first of two visits she made to Jersey Picture: John Le Capelain

many years. A manifestation of the Bailiff achieving mastery is that his chair in the States is set inches higher than that of the Governor's.

In 1627, Sir Philippe de Carteret, Seigneur of St Ouen, became Bailiff and, later, Lieutenant-Governor as well. His first task was to set about improving the defences of the Island. However, though able, his desire to promote his family led him into bitter rivalries with his contemporaries. These rivalries led to factions developing which pulled Jersey into the English Civil War.

When Charles I in 1642 entered into the Civil War with Parliament, Jersey hoped to remain neutral. It had no grievance against the King; in fact the Stuarts had confirmed the Island's privileges and the affairs of the English Parliament were not relevant to the people of Jersey.

Instinctively, however, the majority of Jerseymen sympathised with the English Puritans and the Guernsey Parliamentarians — as much for fear that Catholicism might be reintroduced as to seek revenge on the 15 years of autocratic rule imposed by Sir Philippe de Carteret.

The man who made neutrality impossible was Sir Philippe's nephew, Sir George Carteret, a captain in the Royal Navy. He was given the task by the Royalists of supplying munitions from France. Sir George set sail and attacked merchantmen on their way up the Channel to Parliamentarian London, selling their vessels in St Malo and purchasing arms with the proceeds.

He then came to Jersey to commandeer ammunition and was supported by his uncle. The Rubicon had been crossed and the Island entered into its own civil war.

Parliament elected its own Governor who took up his appointment in St Helier whilst the Royalists held Mont Orgueil. The Island disintegrated into lawlessness and internecine warfare.

In 1643, his uncle having died in Elizabeth Castle during the siege, Sir George Carteret assembled all the troops he could muster, landed at Mont Orgueil and recovered the Island for the King. He became both Bailiff and Lieutenant-Governor and, sensibly using the States as his ally, summoned the population to swear fealty to the King. However, the islanders would only pay lip service to the Royalist cause and would not fight for the King.

Sir George Carteret

To raise funds, Carteret formed his own pirate fleet to hound enemy shipping in the English Channel. He was so successful as a pirate that the King appointed him Vice-Admiral of Jersey, so incorporating his vessels into the Royal Navy.

A spasm of loyalty was awakened by the visit in 1646 of Charles, the young Prince of Wales, who arrived with 300 retainers. He stayed for two months — to the great expense of Carteret and the loyal seigneurs. The Island now had four years' respite and life became almost normal. The States met fortnightly, the Court weekly.

Charles I was executed in 1649. Jersey immediately declared his son Charles King — the first place to do so — and Charles returned to Jersey for six months from September 1649, where he was acknowledged only by Jersey and Scotland as the rightful King of

Elizabeth Castle, St Helier

England and Scotland. He was not to be crowned King in England until the Restoration in 1660.

In 1651 Admiral Blake and Colonel James Heane set sail to capture Jersey. One by one positions capitulated including, on the 27th of October, Mont Orgueil; Heane offering extremely generous terms to the defenders. Elizabeth Castle, now the last heavily defended position of Carteret, would have to be taken. Heane realised that the only way to bring the castle to submission was through gunnery but his cannons were not strong enough to inflict serious damage on the Castle.

It was at this stage in the confrontation that three of the latest weapon, the giant mortar, were sent for from Portsmouth and installed at the foot of Town Hill. On the third shot, a bomb containing 40 lbs of powder landed on the old abbey church, the castle's munitions store. The effect was devastating.

The abbey and adjoining building were destroyed, two thirds of Carteret's provisions were lost and 40 casualties sustained.

Carteret fought on but on the 5th of December, accepting the inevitable, he entered into eight days of negotiation over the terms of surrender. On the 15th the garrison marched out. The siege that had lasted 50 days was over.

The Island was put under military rule, Carteret having successfully negotiated the tenure of all his lands including his gift from Charles in the Americas which became known as New Jersey.

He departed to France where he became an admiral in the French Navy. After the Restoration of the monarchy, Carteret was rewarded by the King and restored to his positions of authority in the English Court.

Subsequently, Jersey was to enjoy a period of relative peace and stability and carried out its traditional way of life of agriculture, marine activities and knitting for almost a century until the Napoleonic wars.

From the Restoration to the End of the Napoleonic Wars

JERSEY'S maritime interests were expanding dramatically. In times of war, Jersey privateers harassed French shipping. In periods of peace, Jersey found a new activity — smuggling.

In 1669 work began on building the harbour at St Aubin, paid for by duties levied on wines and spirits, as the smaller harbours in St Helier could no longer cope with the larger vessels in use. This income from duties was supplemented in 1750 with the introduction of a States lottery.

Farming methods were continually being improved and it was in this period that the trench plough, called in Jèrriais la grande tchéthue, was introduced. This plough required two oxen and six to eight horses to pull it but it reduced the amount of labour involved as well as the number of ploughings. Its effect was a considerable increase in crop yield.

Cider continued to be a major source of income to the farming community, the product being exported widely to, among others, the British Navy.

Under the early Stuarts, the development of the Newfoundland fisheries, the great cod seas, had stagnated but, with the restoration of the monarchy, Jersey merchant men and seamen returned to this hazardous but profitable trade. Many of the merchants became prosperous, the result being the construction of their new homes, known locally as the 'Cod Houses'. Further, through merchant activities, families began to establish businesses not only on the Island but in London and the southern ports.

In 1768, the Chamber of Commerce was formed by the merchants, the first in the British Isles. It is interesting to note that the minutes were written in English although the farming community continued with Jersey French as their first language.

The 18th century saw two public expressions of dissatisfaction. The first, in 1735, was when the local currency was devalued and the sec-

La grande tchéthue or trench plough

ond, in 1769, was in protest against injustices and the failure of the States to regulate a fair price for corn. On both occasions the Jurats had to take refuge in Elizabeth Castle to escape the disgruntled rioters.

Jerseymen have always taken their grievances to the Privy Council on appeal from the local Court and, in response to a petition of 1769, a Lieutenant-Governor was appointed to examine local laws. As a result, the Laws of Jersey were collected and published as a Code in 1771 and approved by the Privy Council 'so that no man need be in ignorance of his rights'.

The power to enact new laws, subject to the sanction of the Privy Council, was conferred upon the States. The Royal Court which, in the past, had from time to time issued ordinances although it had never assumed the power to alter customary law, had this ability removed. However, the Royal Court enrols these new laws once they have been approved by the Crown in Council.

In 1773 France joined America in its war of Independence against England. Jersey's privateering activities were renewed with vigour. As a result, France again tried to conquer Jersey, first in 1779 and, more dramatically, in 1781.

John Wesley, by Nathaniel Hone

In that year Baron De Rullecourt landed at La Rocque with a force of 600 men, marched to St Helier and captured the Lieutenant-Governor, Moise Corbet, convincing him that the French force was superior. The Lieutenant-Governor signed the order for his troops to lay down their arms. His British officers and the Militia, however, refused to accept the surrender claiming that they would rather die than surrender.

Under the command of Major Peirson, the Battle of Jersey was fought in the Royal Square of St Helier. Tragically, both Peirson and De Rullecourt were killed but the Jersey Militia and the British troops won the day.

Jersey now entered into a period of enthusiastic political activity. Two parties were formed, the Jeannots (later to be the Magots) who were Liberals led by John (later Sir John) Dumaresq, and the Charlots or Conservatives, led by Charles Lemprière. The bitter rivalry between the two, which divided the Island's population, was to sully local history for a hundred years until the party system was abandoned in 1891. Since then, party politics have played no major

Detail from the Death of Major Peirson, by J. S. Copley

General George Don

rôle in Jersey government. By this time, the spread of Methodism was greatly encouraged by the arrival of John Wesley who preached his faith in the Island in 1787. The lack of ceremony, the discipline and the austerity of Methodism appealed to the character of many Jersey people who had been used to Calvinism and, although the movement initially met with resistance, it did establish itself throughout the Island.

France declared war on England in 1793 and the French Revolution precipitated a flood of French Royalist refugees and priests to the Island. They were to set up a Royalist spy network operating from Mont Orgueil. Island-wide defensive measures were implemented. In 1806, work began on St Helier's major fort, Fort Regent, where the common land on top of Town Hill had been compulsorily purchased for the new fort. Work had previously begun on the erection of a chain of round, stone towers round the coastline, many of which still stand today. In 1806 General Don became Lieutenant-Governor.

He was a man of immense vigour who introduced a signalling system and put his army on a war footing. His greatest achievement, often against the wishes of parishes and property owners, was the introduction of a network of main roads to facilitate troop movements across Jersey. It is difficult now to imagine, but there was no road across the sweep of the main bay between St Helier and St Aubin, traffic going by boat or using the sands when the tide allowed, until General Don built one.

Privateering was so rife against French shipping that Napoleon stated: 'No. France can tolerate no longer this nest of brigands and assassins. Europe must be purged of this vermin. Jersey is England's shame'. Due to his own defeat at the hands of Wellington at Waterloo in 1815, he was never able to carry out his threat.

With the defeat of Napoleon, the wars with France which had bedevilled English and Jersey history since William the Conqueror, were over. Jersey's position as an outpost of military activity was also at an end.

The stocking trade, for centuries a major source of revenue, had been restricted by the wars but was now to decline through changes in fashion. Cider production, the other major source of income, was also in decline through the mass production of beer. The wars with the French and the two major sources of income had, like the era itself, come to an end.

The Victorian Era

IN 'A Picture of Jersey' written by John Stead in 1809, he was much impressed with the people of Jersey. He describes them as courteous, hospitable, clean and virtuous. He remarks on both the dexterity of the women at knitting and the honesty of the merchants.

He paints an attractive picture where the farmers till fertile fields amid stone cottages, where flowers and crops flourish, where granite manors decorate the parishes and where the pleasures of private concerts and an independent life style are enjoyed.

He also found that the cost of living was low, about half of what it was in any similar place in England. This factor was to attract many English army and navy officers, retired on half pay after the Napoleonic Wars, to settle in Jersey. The agricultural depression in England, and later the famine in Ireland, also encouraged many emigrants to the Island. In 1821 the population was 28,855, but it was to rise dramatically to 37,155 by 1851.

The English influence was most strongly felt in the town of St Helier, although it spread throughout the Island and played an important role in the changes in the social, political and legal life of the Island. St Helier developed rapidly and the architecture of the period reflects the taste of the English residents. Farm labourers came on a seasonal basis from Brittany and Normandy and then began settling in the Island. This migration was to continue until the 1960s, when Portuguese labourers, mainly from Madeira, took their place.

Politically, the Island was divided by the Liberals and Conservatives who had become known as the Rose and the Laurel parties. The bitter rivalries were such that at one election voters were abducted and put on Les Écréhous islets so that they could not cast their vote. Houses were painted in the respective colours and rose or laurel bushes planted in the gardens.

In 1834 Jersey's currency was changed from its historic French livre tournois to the English pound sterling, although parity was not introduced until 1877.

The paddle steamer 'Watersprite', 1830

The language of the Church, States and the Court continued to be French, the language of the fields Jèrriais but the language of commerce, the military, the gentry and the new immigrants was English.

In 1840 the railway from London reached Southampton to connect with the steamships which had started regular services to the Channel Islands in 1827, 13 years before. This facilitated not only trade but encouraged the tourism industry.

Jersey's agriculture, which had seen a decline in its cider production, was to suffer another blow. With the repeal of the Corn Laws, Jersey's main crop of cereals lost its value. Jersey had to find an alternative. Fortunately, it did — in potatoes.

Two farmers were to be instrumental in the development of Jersey's most important modern agricultural crop, the humble potato. The first was John Lecaudey. In those days, potatoes were an autumn crop. In 1858 John Lecaudey, a farmer in St Ouen, convinced his colleagues that by a generous fertilisation with guano and the utilisation of south facing soil, potatoes could be harvested in the spring. They were successful and Jersey established the early potato market.

In 1880 a local farmer, Hugh de la Haye, planted the eyes from two giant potatoes that had been rejected for export and which were being exhibited on the counter at Lecaudey and Co.'s store. He took them home, divided them up and planted them. In the spring of 1881, his first crop of round and kidney-shaped potatoes appeared, quite different to other island potatoes. The potato was named the Jersey Royal Fluke, now known as the Jersey Royal. Its success was phenomenal. By 1919 exports were valued at over a million pounds, an enormous amount of money in those days.

The wars with France had caused the development of another agricultural product that, with the jersey, was to become an emblem of the Island.

Until the 19th century, cows were simply a part of farm existence. With a ban on French imports, Colonel Le Couteur, the honorary ADC to Queen Victoria, convinced the farming community to

Harvesting Jersey Royals, 1920

The gentle Jersey cow

improve its own strain. The result was the development of the Jersey cow with its high quality milk yield, its fawn colour, its dark muzzle, appealing eyes and gentle nature. It now enjoys world wide recognition.

The Jersey cow had a further advantage. It deteriorated after a few generations away from its home island. The replacement of the export herds gave the trade the ideal of self-perpetuation.

In Gorey, on the east coast, the oyster industry began to flourish. The harbour was rebuilt, the number of cottages increased and a new Anglican church built to serve the enlarged community. The oyster beds soon became famous but, by 1864, they had been overdredged and destroyed. It had been a profitable but short lived industry — although oysters are now again being farmed off Gorey.

Oyster boats at Gorey, 1865, by J. F. Draper

Commercial wealth also came from two other sources. Jersey maintained its tariff-free position not only with England but with the American Colonies where there were punitive tariffs against non-British goods. Jersey became a centre for the re-export of goods to the Americas.

The importance of this maritime trade to a small island like Jersey cannot be over-emphasised. The cod fishing off Newfoundland had expanded so much that Jersey firms and islanders were well-established both there and in Labrador. The largest firm in the Gaspé peninsula was established by Charles Robin of St Aubin and has only recently ceased trading.

Not only was there the fishing and the trading, there was also the development of mercantile houses and, as a result of this trade, the development of a ship-building industry.

The freedom of the Channel Islands to trade enabled them to build ships with wood imported from Scandinavia and hemp for rope-making from Russia, at a price well below that of the English ship-builders. By 1865 Jersey had become the fifth largest ship-building port in the British Isles, although the development of steel ships heralded the end of the industry on the shores of Jersey.

Beside this agricultural and mercantile activity, poverty and disease were also endemic. Cholera swept the Island in 1832 and 1849.

La Corbière lighthouse

In 1847 there were riots over the price of bread and many of the poor were forced to emigrate, particularly to Australia, New Zealand and Canada.

Through the 19th century, activities which had been sources of wealth to the Island came to an end. Privateering was abolished in 1815, smuggling on any scale ended around the 1840s, oyster farming by 1864 and cod fishing in the late 1880s. However, from the 1820s, immigration and early tourism were beginning to make their mark. The Island could look forward to the development of new sources of income.

Victoria College, St Helier

The spirit of Victorian enterprise did affect the Island and it is in this period that the Post Office — formed in 1784 — began country deliveries (1827); gas light was introduced (1831); a savings bank opened (1835); plans drawn up for a new St Helier harbour (1837); a sewage system introduced to St Helier (1845); Victoria College was built and opened(1852); the telegraph to England introduced (1858); the railway constructed from St Helier to St Aubin (1870); La Corbière lighthouse built (1874); the Jersey Ladies' College was opened in 1880 and, in 1898, telephones were introduced.

Electricity came late to Jersey and was not introduced to St Helier until 1923.

Great excitement was generated in 1846 with the state visit of Queen Victoria. Though lasting only three hours, it was the first documented official visit by a reigning monarch and parishes, where there was no chance that she would visit, erected arches of welcome and splendid floral displays.

The States, in their dealings with the Privy Council, liked to show their independence. In 1852 the Council issued three orders in Council to improve the Island's administration. These orders were to establish a Police Court, a Petty Debts Court and a paid police force.

The Royal Court refused to register these orders and, after 20 months wrangling, the Privy Council revoked them. The States immediately implemented them, so asserting its own right to initiate laws relating to its own internal government.

Politically, the time was for change. In 1854 the appointment of Governor who rarely, if ever, visited, was officially ended. The Lieutenant-Governor became the Crown's official representative.

In 1857 the composition of the States was changed and expanded. The traditional Constables, Jurats and Rectors held their seats but, in addition, 14 Deputies were elected by popular franchise and in 1891 the ballot box was introduced for local elections.

There was still no direct taxation. The Island's income was raised from duty on wines and spirits, harbour dues, taverners' licences and the letting of market stalls.

In 1900 English was allowed for the first time in debates in the States.

Post Victoria and the Two World Wars

THE political reforms begun in the Victorian era continued to be introduced. In 1907 the number of Deputies was increased from the three for St Helier to six, reflecting the growth of the capital's population. In the same year, elementary education, which had been made compulsory in 1899, was made free.

Agricultural exports, particularly of cows, tomatoes and the lead crop, potatoes, continued as the major source of revenue with the States' income being raised from its local tariffs. At the outbreak of the First World War in 1914, the British garrison was withdrawn and the Jersey Militia mobilised. Over 6,000 Jerseymen fought in the First World War, 862 losing their lives in the conflict. Despite the personal tragedies of this loss of life and further loss in the great influenza epidemic of 1918, the Island remained comparatively undisturbed for the first 40 years of the 20th century.

In 1919 women over 30 were given the vote. A decade later the voting age for women was lowered to 21 and, in 1924, despite die-hard opposition, the States permitted women to sit as Deputies. The die-hards need not have been too alarmed. It was four years before a woman offered herself as a candidate. She was then crushingly defeated. The first woman Deputy, Mrs Ivy Forster, was eventually elected in 1948.

In 1928 the States at last realised that they could not pay their way without direct taxation. Income tax was introduced 'not to exceed a shilling in the pound', i.e. 5 per cent. Travel to the Island was dramatically improved with the arrival in 1934 of the first passenger aeroplane landing on the beach at St Aubin. The beach continued as the airstrip until the opening, in 1937, of the airport in the parish of St Peter. Within the Island, the limited train service was superseded by the bus services and the old tracks were paved over.

At the outbreak of World War Two in 1939, the hope of the islanders was that their experiences of the First World War would be

The control tower Jersey Airport, in the late 1930s

repeated. Too insignificant to bomb, tucked away behind the British Fleet and the Maginot line, the Island in 1940 was advertised in the British press as 'the ideal resort for wartime holidays this summer'.

The collapse of Belgium, the evacuation of Dunkirk and the fall of France meant that the British lines of defence had collapsed and the Germans could reach Cherbourg and St Malo.

Jersey's small craft, marshalled by the St Helier Yacht Club, were involved in their own Dunkirk-style evacuation of troops from France and these troops dug in — the initial plan being to hold the Island. However, the situation worsened and the decision was made by Whitehall to declare the Channel Islands an 'open place' and leave them undefended.

The troops and the total unit of the Royal Militia left to fight from England.

Gorey train station, 1910

The Bailiff, Alexander Coutanche, was sworn in as Civil Governor with the invidious duty, should he have to, of surrendering the Island and making the best terms he could for its inhabitants. He was later created a life peer in recognition of his work during his testing term of office. Meanwhile, the population had to decide whether to stay and face an uncertain future or whether to evacuate. In round figures 10,000 left, many to join the armed forces, and 40,000 stayed.

On the 28th June, 1940, German planes began to bomb and strafe the Island and, on the 1st of July, Alexander Coutanche formally surrendered Jersey to the German High Command. The five years of German Occupation had begun.

The German ultimatum to the Channel Islands on the 1st of July 1940 included the words: 'In case of peaceful surrender the lives, property and liberty of peaceful inhabitants are solemnly guaranteed'. This was a promise, like so many of Hitler's, that was not to be honoured.

On the 16th of September 1942 the first of three deportations in that year began of those who were British born. 1,186 people from

Queues for ration books in St Helier, 1940

Jersey were duly transported to internment camps in Germany. Further deportations were undertaken in January and February 1943, although this time, included alongside those of British birth were others whom the occupiers considered to be 'undesirables'.

The Islanders, despite the desire of the Germans to prove to the world that they were benevolent conquerors, lived under the threat not only of individual punishments but of collective reprisals. 2,600 residents were to be imprisoned for offences against the occupiers, the more serious offenders being deported to concentration camps. A memorial to those who never returned may be found in front of the Jersey Maritime Museum in St Helier.

Under Hitler's direct order an elaborate system of fortifications were built on both Jersey and Guernsey, the remains of many still in evidence today. These fortifications were built by slave labour from countries as widely dispersed as Spain, Russia, Poland and the Ukraine. They lived under the most appalling conditions and islanders who sheltered them when they escaped faced punishment as severe as that meted out to the prisoners themselves.

Cleaning the SK 45 gun barrel, Noirmont, St Brelade

The S.S. Vega in St Helier harbour, 1945

The Jersey administration faced Herculean tasks, one of the most onerous centring on the problem of finance. As well as finding money for its own departments and money for the elderly English population whose pensions no longer reached them it had, under the terms of the Hague Convention, to pay all the expenses of the Army of Occupation — at times as many as 16,000 troops and never less that 10,000.

Income tax was raised to four shillings in the pound or 20 per cent, the rate at which it has been held to the present day.

The banks had money to lend but, by the end of the war, the States were in debt to them to the tune of £6,000,000. This debt was eventually settled by the British government, an act greatly appreciated by the people of Jersey.

Life under the German Occupation is well documented with the period of greatest hardship being in the final year of the war when the Islanders could see that the Allies had liberated neighbouring France. However, for ten months they continued to be besieged by their own fleet and could get no supplies from France.

Without the five visits of the Red Cross ship *Vega*, laden with provisions, it is probable that many would have starved in those last desperate months. As a Jerseyman writing to his daughter at the end of the Occupation explained: 'As you see, we have not died, but we have been very cold and very, very hungry'.

At last, on the 9th of May 1945, following Churchill's declaration the previous day that:'Our dear Channel Islands are to be free today', the German Occupation was over.

To the Present Day

AFTER the Second World War the Island recovered remarkably quickly, with tourism a major contributor to the Treasury and with agriculture reverting back to its successful crops of tomatoes and potatoes and its cattle industry.

However, the social structure in Jersey had altered radically. War veterans, whose parents may have never left the Island, were returning and demanding a better standard of living.

Politically, democracy was recognised by the reform of the States in 1948. Jurats and Rectors lost their automatic right to seats and were replaced by an increase in the number of Deputies (from 17 to 28) elected for a three-year period. Similarly 12 Senators were elected for a six-year period. The Constables retained their right to an *ex officio* seat although this is now also being questioned.

Reforms continued in the legal profession with the legalisation of divorce in 1948, the introduction of a Court of Appeal in 1964 and a Juvenile Court in 1969.

The Constitution of Jersey came under scrutiny in 1969 when a Commission under Lord Crowther attempted to clarify the Island's status. The report's conclusion, published in 1973, remained ambiguous. While accepting that the Crown must have powers to intervene in Island matters, it was unable to specify what those powers should be.

The enigma of Jersey's constitution, based on rights claimed through the events of history, retained its historic status.

In the post-war period, the major problem facing the States was how to fund the infrastructure required to better not only the islanders' desire for a higher standing of living but for the increasing population. Between 1961 and 1971, the population rose from 62,500 to 72,300, of which 6,400 were new immigrants.

In the late 1950s a tax loophole was discovered in the English tax structure whereby death duties could be saved if the money was lent on property mortgages through the Jersey financial and legal system.

The Seigneur of Trinity pays homage to Queen Elizabeth II in 1989

Capital flowed into the Island benefiting the Exchequer and the local legal profession. By 1960 so much money had flowed in that the States approached the British Treasury to stem the flow. By putting its financial relationship with the British Treasury on a more realistic basis, the Island was showing that it wished to prove its probity in financial and tax matters.

In return for the loss of this revenue, the Code of 1771 which disallowed interest rates to exceed 5 per cent was repealed and Jersey's interest rates matched those of the English banks.

Through the 1950s, Jersey established itself as a major banking centre. It offered shelter from UK taxes for those working outside the UK who remitted their sterling earnings to Jersey, and it offered the same lower taxation to British companies which registered themselves in the Island. From this base the 1960s saw the spread of merchant banking and its support industries coming to the Island.

In 1960 deposits totalled £40 million. By 1996 there were 78 deposit-taking institutions holding deposits of £91.6 billion and more than 300 mutual funds managing assets of £31.9 billion.

Including industrial trust assets, the total funds managed in Jersey in 1996 exceeded £200 billion and the industry continues to develop through diversification. From the early days, when it concentrated on deposit-taking and trust and company administration, the finance industry has widened its interests into global custody, treasury operations, security issues, captive insurance, accounting and legal services.

The advantage of this enormous influx of capital is the contribution it can make to Island life, not only in revenue to the Treasury but in employment and by circulation throughout the community. There is, however, the other side of the coin. Success creates enormous pressures on an island such as Jersey, with its limited space and its desire to maintain a balance between its rural attractiveness and the needs for development.

The political stability of the Island, its low taxes, its proximity to London and its sterling currency attracted a new immigrant, the very rich, as well as many well-to-do colonialists who retired to Jersey to avoid punitive British taxes.

One final international hurdle had to be overcome in the 1970s — Jersey's relationship with the European Economic Community. Jersey wished to remain outside the EEC but to receive all the benefits of reduced tariffs throughout the Common Market as it had done with the UK.

Much to everyone's surprise, the Island was successful in obtaining these ends by being recognised as a special case. In return, it had to agree that any advantages enjoyed by UK citizens in the Island would be available to EEC citizens and, conversely, any restrictions on EEC citizens would also apply to UK ones.

Against this political background the Island has thrice been visited by Her Majesty the Queen: in 1957, in 1978 and in 1989. On each occasion, the particular affection that the Islanders have for their sovereign is overtly evident. She is seen, quite correctly, as their liege lord and their special relationship is unhampered by the events of Westminster and her UK Parliament.

Today, the results of the post-war years of stability and prosperity have brought new challenges to the Island's administrators.

**A unique States sitting at Gorey castle in 1996, when the
keys of the castle were handed from the Crown to the Bailiff, who
accepted them on behalf of the Island**

The population has risen to approximately 85,000 through natural increases as well as increases through immigration. The finance industry, farming and the building trade in particular have contributed to these increases as well as the essential and support industries that accompany them. This has put enormous pressure on land and many a landholder has been unable to resist the temptation to sell his land for building purposes. Agriculture is no longer a major contributor to the Island's income and tourism is coming under threat from package holidays to other cheaper and sunnier climates.

The traditional charm of Jersey, its quaintness and its rural attractiveness, are under continuous threat. It is also in danger of pricing itself out of the market for the standard of living in Jersey is higher than anywhere in the UK.

These problems are consequently of the greatest concern to the States of Jersey. The most important question is how to maintain a good standard of living as a stable off-shore tax centre with a balanced economy while not encouraging more immigration. It is the hope of all who live in Jersey that the States can resolve them.

G. R. Balleine concluded his authoritative history of Jersey in 1951 with a quotation from John Oxenham, a writer who set his novels in Sark.

It would seem apt to quote it here as this book owes much to him and to Marguerite Syvret and Joan Stevens upon whose work this brief history is based.

The world is in the melting pot
What was is passing away;
And what will remain when it cools again,
No man can safely say.

THE SOCIÉTÉ JERSIAISE

The Société Jersiaise is an association of over 4000 people from all over the world with a common interest in the pursuit of knowledge about the history, the ancient language, the geology, the natural history and the antiquities of the island of Jersey.

Within the Société, there are 17 sections that specialise in the study of Archives, History, Archaeology, Numismatics, Textile History, Transport and Industrial Archaeology, Geology, Botany, Mycology, Entomology, Marine Biology, Zoology, Ornithology, Garden History, Bibliography, La Langue Jèrriaise and Art and Photographic History. The Société is also concerned with the preservation and conservation of the Island's environment.

The Société not only owns an enormous collection of artifacts which are conserved and exhibited by the Jersey Museums Service but also owns various historical sites around the island including the world renowned site at La Hougue Ble.

At the Société's home at 7 Pier Road, St Helier, are not only the offices and a book shop offering the most comprehensive list of books about the Channel Islands but the second floor houses the Lord Coutanche Library. This Library specialises in both printed and photographic material on Jersey as well as having close links with the Jersey Family History Society.

Each year the Société produces an Annual Bulletin featuring members' specialised research as well as original learned articles. The Société has also a programme of publications, both academic and of general interest, as well as producing for its members two Newsletters each year.

Membership is open to all and an application for membership may be obtained from:

The Société Jersiaise
7 Pier Road
St Helier
Jersey JE2 4XW

Tel: 01534 58314
Fax: 01534 888262

A BRIEF HISTORY OF JERSEY

BIBLIOGRAPHY

The Société Jersiaise has published almost continuously since 1873 an Annual Bulletin. The Bulletins contain an enormous wealth of articles on subjects of Island life. Indexes to the Bulletins and the Bulletins themselves may be found in the Lord Coutanche Library at the Société Jersiaise, 7 Pier Road, St. Helier.

Sources for this book and a selection for further reading are listed below. Dates are of first publication

Ashworth W. S., Historic Jersey, 1993
Backhurst Mrs M., Family History in Jersey, 1991
Bois F. de L., A Constitutional History of Jersey,1970
Bowen E. G., Britain and the Western Seaways, 1972
Briggs Asa, The Channel Islands Occupation & Liberation, 1995
Carey E. F., The Channel Islands, 1904
Chevalier J., A Diary from 1643 to 1651 (in French), 1906
Cruickshank Charles, The German Occupation of the Channel Islands, 1975
Le Dain John, Jersey Alphabet, 1997
Le Feuvre D., Jersey: Not Quite British, 1993
Lemprière Raoul, The Channel Islands, 1970
Messervy Daniel, A Diary from 1762 to 1772 (in French), 1896
Nettles John, Bergerac's Jersey, 1988
Nicolle E. T., A Chronology of Jersey, revised 1954
Reviews of the Channel Island Occupation Society
Rutherford Ward, Jersey, 1976
Spence N. C. W., A Brief History of Jersey, 1993
Syvret M. and Stevens J., Balleine's History of Jersey, 2nd edition, chapter 22, 1998
Vibert Ralph, Memoirs of a Jerseyman, 1991